Pebble®

Families

Aunts

Revised and Updated

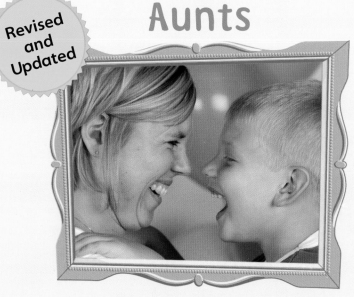

by Lola M. Schaefer

Consulting Editor: Gail Saunders-Smith, PhD

Capstone
press®

Mankato, Minnesota

Pebble Books are published by Capstone Press,
1710 Roe Crest Drive, North Mankato, Minnesota 56003.
www.capstonepress.com

 Books published by Capstone Press are manufactured with paper
containing at least 10 percent post-consumer waste.

Library of Congress Cataloging-in-Publication Data

RECEIVED

DEC 16 2013

Schaefer, Lola M., 1950–
   Aunts/by Lola M. Schaefer. — Rev. and updated.
   p. cm. — (Pebble books. Families)
   Includes bibliographical references and index.
   Summary: "Simple text and photographs present aunts and how they interact with
their families" — Provided by publisher.
   ISBN-13: 978-1-4296-1220-3 (hardcover)
   ISBN-10: 1-4296-1220-7 (hardcover)
   ISBN-13: 978-1-4296-1749-9 (softcover)
   ISBN-10: 1-4296-1749-7 (softcover)
   1. Aunts — Juvenile literature. 2. Nieces — Juvenile literature. 3. Nephews —
Juvenile literature. I. Title. II. Series.
HQ759.94.S33 2008
306.87 — dc22   2007027025

Note to Parents and Teachers

The Families set supports national social studies standards related to
identifying family members and their roles in the family. This book
describes and illustrates aunts. The images support early readers in
understanding the text. The repetition of words and phrases helps
early readers learn new words. This book also introduces early
readers to subject-specific vocabulary words, which are defined in
the glossary section. Early readers may need some assistance to read
some words and to use the Table of Contents, Glossary, Read More,
Internet Sites, and Index sections of the book.

Printed in the United States of America in North Mankato, Minnesota.
062012   006765R

Table of Contents

Aunts

Aunts are sisters
of mothers and fathers.

Aunts live nearby
or far away.

Nieces and Nephews

Aunts have nieces
and nephews.

What Aunts Do

Aunt Laura calls
every Sunday.

Aunt Julia comes
to birthday parties.

Aunt Mandy plays cards.

Aunt Ida goes camping.

Aunt Sammy cuddles.

Aunts love.

Glossary

cuddle — to hold someone closely and lovingly in your arms

father — a male parent; your aunt is your father's sister.

mother — a female parent; your aunt is your mother's sister.

nephew — the son of a brother or sister

niece — the daughter of a brother or sister

sister — a girl or a woman who has the same parents as another person

Read More

Coyle, Carmela LaVigna. *Thank You, Aunt Tallulah!* Flagstaff, Ariz.: Rising Moon, 2006.

West, Colin. *Uncle Pat and Auntie Pat.* Read-It! Chapter Books. Minneapolis: Picture Window Books, 2006.

Internet Sites

FactHound offers a safe, fun way to find Internet sites related to this book. All of the sites on FactHound have been researched by our staff.

Here's how:

1. Visit *www.facthound.com*
2. Choose your grade level.
3. Type in this book ID **1429612207** for age-appropriate sites. You may also browse subjects by clicking on letters, or by clicking on pictures and words.
4. Click on the **Fetch It** button.

FactHound will fetch the best sites for you!

Index

Word Count: 42
Grade 1
Early-Intervention Level: 10

Editorial Credits
Sarah L. Schuette, revised edition editor; Kim Brown, revised edition designer

Photo Credits
Capstone Press/Karon Dubke, all